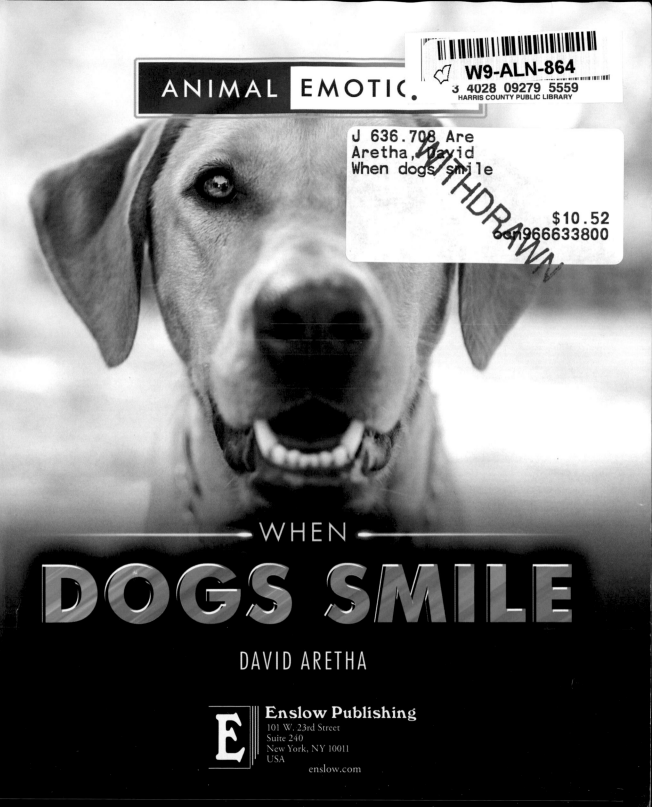

ANIMAL EMOTIO

WHEN
DOGS SMILE

DAVID ARETHA

Enslow Publishing
101 W. 23rd Street
Suite 240
New York, NY 10011
USA

enslow.com

WORDS TO KNOW

agitated Feeling nervous or troubled.

anxiety A feeling of worry or nervousness.

breed A particular kind of dog.

chromosomes Material in a body's cells that carry all of the information used to help a cell grow, thrive, and reproduce.

compassion Concern for a human or other animal.

descended To be a direct blood relative.

domesticated An animal that becomes tame; is kept in a home or on a farm.

evolve To change over a period of time.

motor nerves Nerves that carry signals from the brain to muscles.

sensory nerves Nerves that carry signals to the brain.

CONTENTS

CHAPTER ONE

SIR WIGGLETON'S HAPPY GRIN

In 2016, a big white dog roamed the streets of Detroit, Michigan. The poor pup had no home, and he later spent three months in an animal shelter. That's when Detroit Dog Rescue came to his aid. The group members named the dog Sir Wiggleton, and they took a photo of his huge grin.

The corners of Sir Wiggleton's mouth turned upward—like the Joker in a Batman cartoon. His

It Might Not Be a Smile!

When a dog bares its teeth, it may appear to be smiling. However, it could be agitated and displaying a warning: back off! In such cases, a dog may attempt to snap or bite.

If a dog looks like he's smiling *and* his tongue is hanging out, he likely is happy or excited.

tongue jutted out of his mouth, and his ears perked up. Recalled Kristina Rinaldi of Detroit Dog Rescue, "He had a sparkle in his eye that he needed to get out."

Sir Wiggleton's special smile warmed the heart of musician Dan Tillery. He adopted the dog and renamed him Diggy. "Every time I see him, I get a big dumb smile," Tillery said. "And every time he sees me, he gets a big dumb smile."

A dog's smile can indicate happiness and excitement. Scientists believe dogs experience other emotions, too. They include sadness, **anxiety**, fear, and anger. Dogs also show **compassion** to humans as well as the most special emotion: love.

CHAPTER TWO

DESCENDED FROM WOLVES

Scientists have no doubt that dogs **descended** from wolves. Dogs and wolves have the same biological "make-up." In fact, wolves and dogs have the exact same seventy-eight **chromosomes**.

Yet, we all know that wolves are different than dogs. Wolves live in forests and are afraid to get near people. And people are afraid of wolves. Wolves kill and eat large animals, like elk and moose. They

Friendly Fidos

DogTime lists the "friendliest" dog breeds. They include bichon frise, golden retriever, Irish setter, Labrador retriever, and others. These breeds are friendly with family, children, strangers, and other dogs.

sometimes attack and kill humans, too. They are very different than cute, fluffy poodles!

Some wolves started to be **domesticated** around 15,000 years ago. That means they started living comfortably with people. Biologist Raymond

The golden retriever (*left*) still bears resemblance to wolves, including this gray wolf.

Coppinger believes that these wolves were attracted to the humans' food. Over thousands of years, the wolves

Fact

There are 167 breeds of dogs, according to the American Kennel Club.

who stayed with people **evolved** into domesticated dogs. Wolves in the forest stayed the same, but domesticated dogs changed a lot. Some **breeds** of dogs are big. Others are small. But they all are pals with their human owners.

Wolves strongly desire to stay with their pack—a group of fellow wolves. Dogs are also pack animals, but their pack includes their human family. They're happy when the family is together. They can be sad and anxious when left alone. Some dogs get so lonely that they howl...just like a wolf.

CHAPTER THREE

ALWAYS HAPPY TO SEE YOU

In the animated move *The Secret Life of Pets*, Max is an adorable Jack Russell terrier. He spends his days waiting for his owner, Katie, to come home. When she finally arrives, he transforms into "happy" mode. His ears perk up. His eyes brighten. He beams a smile. He sticks out his tongue and pants.

But that's not all. Happy Max barks excitedly. He wags his tail. He leaps up toward Katie. And he kisses her face. He is one joyful dog!

Ticklish Rats?

Jaak Panksepp, a neuroscientist, said that other animals make happy noises, too. Even rats! Panksepp tickled the necks of rats and found that they chirped joyfully.

Real dogs act much like Max. Some big dogs stand on their hind legs, and they put their front legs on their owner's shoulders. Then they give their owner a big, sloppy lick! If they haven't seen their owner in many days, dogs are *extra* thrilled to see them. They can be so happy that they cry. Soldiers who come home from overseas often get the biggest greetings. Dogs cry and lick their faces because they haven't seen them in months.

Scientist Patricia Simonet said dogs make a certain panting sound when they're happy. When they are tired or thirsty, their pant is like, "Huh-huh, huh-huh, huh-huh,

Dogs are happiest with their family. They can't wait for their owners to return.

When owners return after being gone for months, their dogs are often overcome with emotion.

Fact

Almost all mammals use a facial expression when they are trying to be friendly.

huh-huh." But their happy pant sounds like, "Ha-huh! Ha-huh! Ha-huh! Ha-huh!"

Play with your dog and see if they make that happy noise!

CHAPTER FOUR

READING A DOG'S MIND

For thousands of years, people have wondered what their dog is thinking. You can ask your dog, "Hey, what are you thinking?" But the most he'll respond is, "Ruff!" Now, scientists are starting to read dogs' minds.

Researchers have proven that dogs are happy to see their owners. In 2014, scientists at Emory

Superior Sense of Smell

A human brain is about 10 times larger than a dog's brain. However, the part of the dog's brain that controls smell is about 40 times larger than the same part of a human brain. That's why dogs have a much greater sense of smell than people.

According to most scientists, dogs—including this English springer spaniel—are among the smartest animals.

University in Georgia staged a cool experiment. They used a functional magnetic resonance imaging

Fact

Many experts believe that dogs are as smart as two-year-old humans.

(fMRI) machine to examine dogs' brains. They focused on the caudate nucleus, a part of the brain known as the "reward center."

The scientists introduced different scents to each dog. Their fMRI machine determined that the scent of the dog's owner stimulated *a lot* of activity in the doggy brain's "reward center."

When the dog's caudate nucleus is stimulated, the dog enters happy mode. Scientifically, this is how it works: When owner comes home, the dog's **sensory nerves** take this message to the brain. The brain's caudate nucleus is immediately activated. This activation triggers the dog's **motor nerves**. The motor nerves stimulate muscles to act in a certain way.

This boy is activating the dog's caudate nucleus. And the dog is doing the same for the boy!

These nerves turn up the facial muscles. They perk up the ear muscles. They wag the tail muscles. And so on.

A human's nervous system works the same way. Except for one thing: We don't have a tail!

CHAPTER FIVE

WHAT GIVES A DOG JOY

"Rover, we're going to the park for a picnic!"

Yeeaaayyy! Rover says in his mind.

A picnic at the park includes everything that makes Rover happy and smiley. First, he gets to go with his favorite people: his family. If he's a big dog, he probably will like the car ride to the park. Dogs enjoy the breeze when their head is out the window. They also like staring at all the different things they pass on the road.

Dogs on the Go

You can take your dog with you on vacation. There are thousands of pet-friendly motels in the United States. Some charge a fee, while others don't. But if your dog pees on the carpet, your family will have to pay the clean-up fee!

Dogs enjoy sticking their head out the car window, but the wind can dry their eyes, and they could fall out of the car.

At the park, Rover loves the thrill of running around. If you throw a ball or a stick, he'll enjoy retrieving it. This is especially true if he's a retriever, such as a golden retriever or Labrador retriever.

At the park, he likely will meet other dogs. Most dogs like to meet and play with other dogs. Sometimes they'll run around together or wrestle playfully. Rover is also interested in sniffing the park's many scents.

Back at the picnic table, Rover might enjoy a nice tummy rub. The hand feels good on his skin, like when we get a massage. Of course, a tasty meal will make Rover happy. Dogs are carnivores, meaning they crave meat. Burgers, hot dogs, a bucket of fried chicken…. Mmmm! It all sounds good to Rover!

After the picnic, Rover is glad to go back to his favorite place: home. He has enjoyed a day filled with smiles, happy panting, and tail wags. And now he drifts blissfully off to sleep....

Dogs enjoy playing with one another at the park just as much as kids like playing with their friends.

CHAPTER SIX

WHY THEY DO WHAT THEY DO

Why do dogs do all the silly things they do? Well, that depends on what they're doing.

First of all, dogs respond to food. People use food to train dogs to do tricks. For a treat, dogs will learn to roll over or "play dead." They'll even learn to run through an obstacle course if rewarded with bits of food.

And why do retriever dogs love to chase things? Centuries ago, people trained dogs to hunt. After the

Chew on This

Why do puppies chew on toys, shoes, and furniture? It's their way of relieving pain caused by incoming teeth. Older dogs chew to keep their teeth clean and jaws strong.

This dog is willing to learn a new lesson in order to get that tasty treat.

hunter shot a bird or small animal, their retriever was trained to go get the animal and bring it to them. Retriever dogs aren't used much for hunting anymore.

Retrievers, including this Labrador retriever, are best at fetching and returning things.

But, they still have the instinct to go retrieve things, like balls and sticks.

    All dogs like to sniff things. They sniff other dogs,

Fact

Many types of dogs kill small animals, like mice and rabbits, and bring them to their owners as a "gift."

trees, humans, plants, and more. Why do they sniff so much? Experts say it's because they have powerful noses. A dog can smell many more scents than a human. Dogs seem to be amazed and delighted by this variety of scents. It's like how we're dazzled by a colorful animated movie.

CHAPTER SEVEN

A DOG'S MANY EMOTIONS

In the movie *Because of Winn-Dixie*, the dog Winn-Dixie is afraid of thunder. During a storm, he runs around barking like crazy. The poor dog is nervous. Nervousness, or anxiety, is one of many emotions a dog experiences.

Nervous dogs act unusually. Their heart beats faster. Their eyes grow wide and their ears may perk up. They may pant, bark, or run around. They

Not Guilty

Some dogs express a guilty look after committing a "no-no" — like pooping on the floor. But dog psychologists believe that dogs do not feel guilt. They are just concerned that their owners will punish them.

This dalmatian looks guilty. However, she probably is just afraid that her owner might be mad at her.

are more likely to pee or poop. They may become aggressive and destructive. They may try to leave or hide under the couch.

Dogs become sad when someone they love leaves. It could be a person, another dog, or even another animal friend. When a dog is sad, its eyes, ears, and tail all droop. They tend to plop on the floor and lie there for a long time. They lose their appetite.

This Jack Russell terrier is definitely in "angry mode"! Look at her teeth and stance.

Sometimes, dogs get mad. They're very protective of their food, their loved ones, and their home. If any of

Fact

Dogs experience simple emotions, but not complex ones. For example, they do not experience pride, shame, or envy.

those are threatened, they'll enter "angry mode." The dog's muscles tense up. She bares her teeth. She barks as loudly as she can.

Dogs are compassionate, loving animals. A loving dog will cuddle up against you. He'll place his paw in your hand or his chin on your lap. He'll lick your face—which is like giving you a kiss. If you cry sad tears, he'll lick them away. He just wants to make you feel better.

CHAPTER EIGHT

HOW DOGS ARE LIKE US

People don't look like dogs *at all*. But we do express emotions similar to our furry pals.

Let's start with sadness. Like dogs, our face and eyes droop when we're sad. We lack energy and tend to lie around more. We may even eat less, just like dogs.

When we're joyful, we kind of act like dogs do. Let's say we're watching our favorite football team on TV. When our team scores a touchdown, we jump up and cheer. That's like the dog running and leaping

Hero Dogs

Many dogs have put their lives in danger to save their human family members. In 2016, a dog in Maryland died while protecting a baby during a house fire.

and barking. Our mouths and eyes grow wide, just like Sir Wiggleton's. We don't have tails to wag, but at football games we do wave towels and pom-poms!

In an anxious situation, we're like dogs in a lot of ways. For example, say someone calls to tell us our best friend was in an accident. Our heart beats faster and our breathing becomes heavy. We may start talking loudly, like barking dogs. We start moving around faster, too. If there's a terrible storm outside, we may try to hide in a safe place—just like dogs.

We also express love in

See? Dogs and people really are a lot alike!

Face licks are just like kisses. It's a dog's way of expressing his affection.

Fact

Dogs are some of the only mammals that make eye contact with humans.

a similar way. We hold loved ones close. We wrap our arms around them. We may not lick their face, but we will give them a kiss.

Books

Buchanan, Shelley. *Animal Senses.* Huntington Beach, CA: Teacher Created Materials, 2016.

Hibbert, Clare. *If You Were a Dog.* Mankato, MN: Black Rabbit Books, 2014.

Newman, Aline Alexander. *Animal Superstars: And More True Stories of Amazing Animal Talents.* Washington, DC: National Geographic Society, 2013.

Rustad, Martha. *Dogs.* Chicago: Capstone, 2015.

Websites

Animal Fact Guide

animalfactguide.com/links

Learn about interesting animals from around the world.

Animal Planet/Dogs

animalplanet.com/pets/dogs/

Includes fun facts, tricks you can teach, Puppy Bowl highlights, and much more.

How to Love Your Dog

loveyourdog.com/

This site is a kid's guide to dog care.

Ranger Rick

nwf.org/kids/ranger-rick/animals.aspx

Features lots of animal info from the National Wildlife Federation.

INDEX

Published in 2018 by Enslow Publishing, LLC.
101 W. 23rd Street, Suite 240, New York, NY 10011

Library of Congress Cataloging-in-Publication Data

Names: Aretha, David.
Title: When dogs smile / David Aretha.
Description: New York City : Enslow Publishing, 2018.
| Series: Animal emotions | Includes bibliographical references and index. | Audience:
  Grades 1 to 3.
Identifiers: LCCN 2016057566 | ISBN 9780766086135 (library bound : alk. paper) | ISBN 9780766088627 (pbk.) | ISBN 9780766088566 (6-pack)
Subjects: LCSH: Dogs–Behavior–Juvenile literature. | Dogs–Psychology–Juvenile literature. | Emotions in animals-Juvenile literature.
Classification: LCC SF433 .A734 2017 | DDC 636.7/089689142-dc23
LC record available at https://lccn.loc.gov/2016057566

Printed in the United States of America

To Our Readers: We have done our best to make sure all website addresses in this book were active and appropriate when we went to press. However, the author and the publisher have no control over and assume no liability for the material available on those websites or on any websites they may link to. Any comments or suggestions can be sent by email to customerservice@enslow.com.

Photo Credits: Cover, p. 1 Purple Collar Pet Photography/Moment/Getty Images; pp. 4, 7, 10, 13, 17, 20, 24, 28 Piotr Krzeslak/Shutterstock.com; p. 5 aodaodaodaod/Shutterstock.com; p. 8 Don Johnston/All Canada Photos/Getty Images; p. 11 Thomas Northcut/DigitalVision/Getty Images; p. 12 Catherine Ledner/Taxi/Getty Images; p. 14 Matthew Richardson/Alamy Stock Photo; p. 16 Lori Adamski Peek/Photolibrary/Getty Images; p. 18 Maisie Paterson/Stone/Getty Images; p. 19 Hollysdogs/Shutterstock.com; p. 21 Shalom Ormsby/Blend Images/Getty Images; p. 22 Allison Dumas/Alamy Stock Photo; p. 25 Image Source/Photodisc/Getty Images; p. 26 Philip James Corwin/Corbis Documentary/Getty Images; p. 29 SergiyN/Shutterstock.com; p. 30 Elizabethsalleebauer/RooM/Getty Images; interior pages, back cover background image De Space Studio/Shutterstock.com.